Franz LISZT

Les Préludes
Symphonic Poem No. 3
S. 97

Study Score
Partitur

PETRUCCI LIBRARY PRESS

INTRODUCTION

The present score is a reissue of one from the Franz Liszt-Stiftung edition, originally published by Breitkopf & Härtel from 1907-1936. The edition was prepared in an effort to publish the entire oeuvre of Franz Liszt. Editors included such prominent musicians as Béla Bartok, Ferruccio Busoni, Eugène d'Albert and José Vianna da Motta – some of whom studied with Liszt – as well as scholars like Peter Raabe, who would later compile the first catalog of the composer's works. The need for a complete edition was already apparent by the time of Liszt's death. Although some of his piano music had regularly appeared in new editions throughout his life, these works were by no means representative of even his pianistic output. A far more unfortunate fate was left for his orchestral music - which would usually be issued only once, soon to go out of print and later scarcely available. The Liszt-Stiftung edition revived many works that had fallen into relative obscurity and was therefore handsomely welcomed.

The edition was sadly never completed. The publication activity was brought to a premature end by the time of the Second World War. All in all the incomplete edition encompassed 34 volumes, among others two symphonies, the symphonic poems, some concert works, a couple of piano arrangements and 11 volumes of original works for piano – a mere fraction of the composer's output – but the edition would nonetheless break the ground for Liszt research during the 20th century for a number of reasons. First, it brought to light a number of late pieces that would put Liszt as a forerunner of experimental music and firmly establish his position as such. Second, it revealed the diversity of Liszt's output, which up until that time had been best known as an important addition to the piano repertoire. Third, it displayed the complex and characteristic nature of many of his works by being the first edition to show and make use of several alternative (sometimes vastly different) versions and sources. Last but not least, it would provide the world with a generally reliable edition of easy availability and very high standard for its day.

The Bavarian State Library acquired a complete copy of said edition and decided to digitize it in 2008. By that time more than 70 years had passed since its publication, effectively rendering the edition out of copyright and free for any use. Each and every page was scanned and uploaded to their online digital collection. While this was a great effort in itself, the site has a rudimentary interface, is difficult to navigate and the scores are not in the context of relevant information. One of our users decided to also upload it to our site, the International Music Score Library Project (IMSLP) / Petrucci Music Library, the unique wiki-based repository of musical scores, composers and indexes that anyone can edit and amend. Through the effort of a single user, Mattias K. (piupianissimo), the entire edition is now easily available worldwide to those who wish to perform and study the composer's music in a historical context, since as the case is with Liszt's music, many early editions exist and many are readily available on the site and many more will be available in the future. IMSLP is as such a valuable resource available to the scholar but even more to the performer who is always a mere mouse click away from scores that have not been in print since the turn of the past century, or that are otherwise hard to come by. The availability, quantity of ease of access for online scores will soon exceed those of the traditional medium of print. Nevertheless new works have always been published through the printed medium and this tradition is going to persist for many years to come even if complemented by the digital medium. Of course an important fact to stress is that the availability of digital scores online does not exclude the need of printed score since neither one can replace the comfort and neatness of one another. The quality of a bound reprint or new engraving exceeds that of a score printed at home.

I discovered IMSLP back in early 2006 when it first began. At that time many scores were scattered on the net either privately or on commercial collection sites. Many of these sites had a considerably large collection but sadly many had restrictions on number of downloads per day and the process of contributing to them was riddled with bureaucracy. IMSLP was the first free site where anyone could contribute and upload any kind of musical scores. I have personally searched and uploaded many works – particularly those of Liszt – and the future of the site is nothing but bright. At the time of its start only a handful of scores were available on the site but through the effort of its users IMSLP has grown to be the largest collection of scores available on the Internet.

Les Préludes is the third work in a series of thirteen symphonic poems composed by Franz Liszt. It was composed from 1850-55 and first published in 1856 by Breitkopf und Härtel of Leipzig. The dedicatee is Princess Carolyne zu Sayn-Wittgenstein. This score is from the second volume of the Franz Liszt-Stiftung edition, edited by Otto Taubmann and published in 1908. The score, along with a number or arrangements, is also available directly at the following URL:
http://imslp.org/wiki/Les_préludes,_S.97_(Liszt,_Franz)

Soren Afshar (Funper)

Summer, 2011

PRÄLUDIEN

NACH LAMARTINE.

SYMPHONISCHE DICHTUNG No. 3 VON F. LISZT.

Was andres ist unser Leben, als eine Reihenfolge von Präludien zu jenem unbekannten Gesang, dessen erste und feierliche Note der Tod anstimmt? Die Liebe ist das leuchtende Frührot jedes Herzens; in welchem Geschick aber wurden nicht die ersten Wonnen des Glücks von dem Brausen des Sturmes unterbrochen, der mit rauhem Odem seine holden Illusionen verweht, mit tödlichem Blitz seinen Altar zerstört, — und welche, im Innersten verwundete Seele suchte nicht gern nach solchen Erschütterungen in der lieblichen Stille des Landlebens die eignen Erinnerungen einzuwiegen? Dennoch trägt der Mann nicht lange die wohlige Ruhe inmitten besänftigender Naturstimmungen, und „wenn der Drommete Sturmsignal ertönt", eilt er, wie immer der Krieg heissen möge, der ihn in die Reihen der Streitenden ruft, auf den gefahrvollsten Posten, um im Gedränge des Kampfes wieder zum ganzen Bewußtwerden seiner selbst und in den vollen Besitz seiner Kraft zu gelangen.

(Uebers. v. P. Cornelius.)

LES PRÉLUDES

D'APRÈS LAMARTINE*

POÈME SYMPHONIQUE No. 3 DE F. LISZT.

Notre vie est-elle autre chose qu'une série de Préludes à ce chant inconnu dont la mort entonne la première et solennelle note? — L'amour forme l'aurore enchantée de toute existence; mais quelle est la destinée où les premières voluptés du bonheur ne sont point interrompues par quelque orage, dont le souffle mortel dissipe ses belles illusions, dont la foudre fatale consume son autel, et quelle est l'âme cruellement blessée qui, au sortir d'une de ces tempêtes, ne cherche à reposer ses souvenirs dans le calme si doux de la vie des champs? Cependant l'homme ne se résigne guère à goûter longtemps la bienfaisante tiédeur qui l'a d'abord charmé au sein de la nature, et lorsque «la trompette a jeté le signal des alarmes», il court au poste périlleux quelle que soit la guerre qui l'appelle à ses rangs, afin de retrouver dans le combat la pleine conscience de lui-même et l'entière possession de ses forces.

*) Méditations poétiques.

THE PRELUDES

AFTER LAMARTINE'S "MÉDITATIONS POÉTIQUES"

SYMPHONIC POEM No. 3 BY F. LISZT.

What else is our life but a series of preludes to that unknown Hymn, the first and solemn note of which is intoned by Death? — Love is the glowing dawn of all existence; but what is the fate where the first delights of happiness are not interrupted by some storm, the mortal blast of which dissipates its fine illusions, the fatal lightning of which consumes its altar; and where in the cruelly wounded soul which, on issuing from one of these tempests, does not endeavor to rest his recollection in the calm serenity of life in the fields? Nevertheless man hardly gives himself up for long to the enjoyment of the beneficent stillness which at first he has shared in Nature's bosom, and when "the trumpet sounds the alarm", he hastens, to the dangerous post, whatever the war may be, which calls him to its ranks, in order at last to recover in the combat full consciousness of himself and entire possession of his energy.

COMPOSER'S PREFACE

Eine Aufführung, welche den Intentionen des Komponisten entsprechen und ihnen Klang, Farbe, Rhythmus und Leben verleihen soll, wird bei meinen Orchester-Werken am zweckmässigsten und mit dem geringsten Zeitverlust durch geteilte Vor-Proben gefördert werden. Demzufolge erlaube ich mir, die HH. Dirigenten, welche meine symphonischen Dichtungen aufzuführen beabsichtigen, zu ersuchen, der General-Probe Separat-Proben mit dem Streich-Quartett, andere mit Blas- und Schlag-Instrumenten vorangehen zu lassen.

Gleichzeitig sei mir gestattet zu bemerken, dass ich das mechanische, taktmässige, zerschnittene Auf- und Abspielen, wie es an manchen Orten noch üblich ist, möglichst beseitigt wünsche, und nur den periodischen Vortrag, mit dem Hervortreten der besonderen Accente und der Abrundung der melodischen und rhythmischen Nuanzierung, als sachgemäss anerkennen kann. In der geistigen Auffassung des Dirigenten liegt der Lebensnerv einer symphonischen Produktion, vorausgesetzt, dass im Orchester die geziemenden Mittel zu deren Verwirklichung sich vorfinden; andernfalls möchte es ratsamer erscheinen, sich nicht mit Werken zu befassen, welche keineswegs eine Alltags-Popularität beanspruchen.

Obschon ich bemüht war, durch genaue Anzeichnungen meine Intentionen zu verdeutlichen, so verhehle ich doch nicht, dass Manches, ja sogar das Wesentlichste, sich nicht zu Papier bringen lässt, und nur durch das künstlerische Vermögen, durch sympathisch schwungvolles Reproduzieren, sowohl des Dirigenten als der Aufführenden, zur durchgreifenden Wirkung gelangen kann. Dem Wohlwollen meiner Kunstgenossen sei es daher überlassen, das Meiste und Vorzüglichste an meinen Werken zu vollbringen.

Weimar, März 1856.

Pour obtenir un résultat d'exécution correspondant aux intentions de mes œuvres orchestrales, et leur donner le coloris, le rhythme, l'accent et la vie qu'elles réclament, il sera utile d'en préparer la répétition générale par des répétitions partielles des instruments à cordes, à vent, en cuivre, et à percussion. Par cette méthode de la division du travail on épargnera du temps en facilitant aux exécutants l'intelligence de l'ouvrage. Je me permets en conséquence de prier MM. les chefs d'orchestre qui seraient disposés à faire exécuter l'un de ces Poèmes symphoniques, de vouloir bien prendre le soin de faire précéder les répétitions générales, des répétitions préalables indiquées ci-dessus.

En même temps j'observerai que la mesure dans les œuvres de ce genre demande à être maniée avec plus de mesure, de souplesse, et d'intelligence des effets de coloris, de rhythme, et d'expression qu'il n'est encore d'usage dans beaucoup d'orchestres. Il ne suffit pas qu'une composition soit régulièrement bâtonnée et machinalement exécutée avec plus ou moins de correction pour que l'auteur ait à se louer de cette façon de propagation de son œuvre, et puisse y reconnaître une fidèle interprétation de sa pensée. Le nerf vital d'une belle exécution symphonique gît principalement dans la compréhension de l'œuvre reproduite, que le chef d'orchestre doit surtout posséder et communiquer, dans la manière de partager et d'accentuer les périodes, d'accuser les contrastes tout en ménageant les transitions de veiller tantôt à établir l'équilibre entre les divers instruments, tantôt à les faire ressortir soit isolément soit par groupes, car à tel moment il convient d'entonner ou de marquer simplement les notes, mais à d'autres il s'agit de phraser, de chanter, et même de déclamer. C'est au chef qu'il appartient d'indiquer à chacun des membres de l'orchestre la signification du rôle qu'il a à remplir.

Je me suis attaché à rendre mes intentions par rapport aux nuances, à l'accélération et au retard des mouvements, etc. aussi sensibles que possible par un emploi détaillé des signes et des expressions usitées; néanmoins ce serait une illusion de croire qu'on puisse fixer sur le papier ce qui fait la beauté et le caractère de l'exécution. Le talent et l'inspiration des artistes dirigeants et exécutants en ont seuls le secret, et la part de sympathie que ceux-ci voudront bien accorder à mes œuvres, seront pour elles le meilleur gage de succès.

Weimar, Mars 1856.

In order to secure a performance of my orchestral works which accords with their intentions, and which imparts to them the colour, rhythm, accent and life that they require, it is recommended that the general rehearsal should be preceded by separate rehearsals of the Strings, Wind, Brass, and instruments of percussion. By this division of labour time will be saved, and the executants will more rapidly be made familiar with what is required of them. I therefore venture to request that conductors, who are pleased to bring one or the other of my symphonic poems to a hearing will adopt the plan formulated above.

At the same time I may be allowed to remark that it is my wish that the mechanical, bar by bar, up and down beating of time, which obtains in so many places, should as far as possible be discarded, and that only the periodic divisions, with the prominence of certain accentuation and the rounding off of melodic and rhythmical nuances should alone be regarded as indispensable. The vitality of a symphonic performance depends upon the intellectual perception of the conductor, presuming that suitable material for its realisation is to be found in the orchestra; failing this it would seem to be advisable to hold aloof from works which do not claim a promise of every-day popularity.

Although I have endeavoured to make my intentions clear by providing exact marks of expression, I cannot conceal from myself that much, and that perhaps the most important, cannot be set forth on paper, but can only be successfully brought to light by the artistic capability and the sympathetic and enthusiastic reproduction by both conductor and executants. It may therefore be left to my colleagues in art to do the most and best that they can for my works.

Weimar, March 1856.

F. Liszt.

INSTRUMENTATION

3 Flutes (3rd also Piccolo)
2 Oboes
2 Clarinets (C)
2 Bassoons

4 Horns (C)
2 Trumpets (C)
3 Trombones
Tuba

Timpani
Percussion
(Snare Drum, Bass Dum, Cymbals)
Harp

Violins I
Violins II
Violas
Violoncellos
Basses

Duration: ca. 16 minutes

First Performance: February 23, 1854
Weimar: Hofkapelle Weimar
Franz Liszt, conductor

ISBN: 978-1-60874-023-9

This score is an unabridged reprint of the score
first issued in Leipzig by Breitkopf & Härtel, 1908. Plate F. L. 3

Printed in the USA
First Printing: November, 2011

Les Préludes

Symphonic Poem No. 3

S. 97

Franz Liszt (1811–1886)

*) Militair-Trommel, Becken, Grosse Trommel treten im letzten Allegro marziale (S. 65) ein.
Military-drum, cymbals and big drum join in the last Allegro marziale.
Tambour militaire, cymbales, grosse caisse jouent au dernier Allegro marziale.

PETRUCCI LIBRARY PRESS

6

Andante maestoso.

Andante maestoso.

40239

7

10

L'istesso tempo.

L'istesso tempo.

40239

14

16

18

20

22

Allegro ma non troppo.

Allegro ma non troppo.

Allegro tempestuoso.

28

30

32

a tempo (agitato)

a tempo (agitato)

34

36

38

44

45

46

48

51

Poco a poco più di moto sino al Allegro marziale.

Poco a poco più di moto sino al Allegro marziale.

40239

54

60

40239

64

66

68

70

BAND 2

TRAUERFEIER TASSOS.
Symphonische Dichtung Nr. 2a.

Vorlage: 1. Die erste Partiturausgabe, erschienen 1878 bei Breitkopf & Härtel in Leipzig. Verlagsnummer 14686.

2. Abschrift im Besitze von Breitkopf & Härtel.

S. 1. Die Anmerkung »Tiefe Glocke oder Tamtam tritt auf Seite 35 ein« steht nicht in der gedruckten Vorlage, sondern ist hinzugefügt worden.

S. 6, 1. Takt (Hörner)
S. 27, 4. Takt (Pauken)
S. 28, 3. Takt (Hörner)
S. 34, 4. Takt (Hörner)
Die Forderung, in den genannten Instrumenten die Stimmung zu wechseln, steht in der gedruckten Vorlage in deutscher Sprache. Es wurde dafür nach den Gepflogenheiten dieser Ausgabe immer das Wort »muta« gesetzt.

* * *

LES PRÉLUDES.
Symphonische Dichtung Nr. 3.*)

Vorlage: 1. Die erste Partiturausgabe, erschienen 1856 bei Breitkopf & Härtel in Leipzig. Verlagsnummer 9056.

2. Die autographe Partitur im Liszt-Museum in Weimar.

S. 2. Die gedruckte Vorlage hat über und unter dem 6. und 7. Takt die Vorschrift »*Poco ritenuto*«; bei den Bläsern folgt dann im 8. und 9. Takt unter jedem System der spielenden Instrumente ein »*più rit. e smorz.*« Gemäß den für die Gesamtausgabe maßgebenden Leitsätzen wurde das »*più rit.*« dieser zuletzt genannten Takte ebenfalls nur über und unter das Gesamtsystem der Partitur gesetzt, während allein die Vorschrift »*smorz.*« unter jeder Bläserzeile verblieb.

---

*) R. Pohl hat in einem in der Neuen Zeitschrift für Musik vom 24./4. 1889 veröffentlichten Artikel eine Reihe Vortragsbezeichnungen und Tempoangaben mitgeteilt, die er auf Grund persönlicher Wahrnehmungen bei der Aufführung der »Préludes« unter des Komponisten eigener Leitung aufgezeichnet, und deren Beachtung er — als die richtige Interpretation des Werkes fördernd — empfiehlt. (Diese Zutaten sind hier aufgenommen und eingeklammert). Es sind die folgenden: (Die Seitenzahlen beziehen sich auf die Gesamtausgabe).

Seite 6. *ritardando — molto ritenuto*. Die Staccato-Punkte fort.
» 9—10. Pauke: Staccato-Punkte fort.
» 17—19. Harfe *mf*, statt *p*.
» 20. *poco a poco accelerando*.
» 29. *molto agitato ed accelerando*, statt nur *molto agitato*.
» 31. *Ritenuto (pesante)*.
» 31—33. *a tempo, ritard., a tempo, riten., a tempo (agitato)*.
» 34—35. Pauke *ff*, statt *f*.
» 41. *Allegro moderato*, eingeklammert.
» 50. *poco a poco più mosso*.
» 60. Violinen *ff*.
» 62. Viol. *p cresc.* usw.
» 64. *poco ritenuto*.
» 65. *Tempo di marcia*.
» 66. *Più maestoso*.
» 68. *Vivace*. (Diese Bezeichnung wurde gewählt um den deutschen Ausdruck »lebhaft« zu vermeiden.)
» 77. *molto ritardando*.

S. 41. Im ersten Takt steht in der gedruckten Vorlage bei den Violoncellen die Bezeichnung »Solo«. Offensichtlich handelt es sich aber nur um den solistischen Vortrag der Stelle durch alle Violoncelle und nicht um deren Wiedergabe durch nur einen Spieler. (Siehe auch auf der nächsten Seite im 5. Takt die Vorschrift »divisi«!)

S. 53. Die gedruckte Vorlage hat im 4. Takt als letzte Achtelnote (Auftakt) der 2. Bratschen ein *h* ! Die Note muß zweifellos *g* heißen, und es dürfte ein Stichfehler vorliegen, der entsprechend verbessert wurde.

* * *

ORPHEUS.
Symphonische Dichtung Nr. 4.

Vorlage: 1. Die erste Partiturausgabe, erschienen 1856 bei Breitkopf & Härtel in Leipzig. Verlagsnummer 9066.

2. Die autographe Partitur im Liszt-Museum in Weimar.

Bemerkungen:

S. 1. In der gedruckten Vorlage steht im Instrumentenvordruck folgende Bezeichnung der vier Hörner: 1 Horn in *F*, 1 Horn in *C*, 2 Hörner in *F*. Da die vorhandenen drei *F*-Hörner damit nicht genügend unterschieden erscheinen, wurde geändert: 1. Horn in *F*, 2. Horn in *C*, 3. und 4. Horn in *F*.

S. 3. Der letzte Takt lautet im 4. Horn in der gedruckten Vorlage ; in den II. Violoncellen steht dagegen . Der Widerspruch, daß die Hörner den Ton *es* halten, während gleichzeitig von den I. Violoncellen die beiden Töne *e-dis* (= *es*) intoniert werden, löst sich, wenn man annimmt, daß es in den Violoncellen heißen soll. Dem entsprechen auch die analogen Stellen auf S. 4, 11. Takt und S. 24, 7. Takt, sowie die Fassung des Klavierarrangements.

S. 25. Im dritten Takt steht in der gedruckten Vorlage zum Einsatz der 1. Trompete ein »*p*« gegen das »*f*« der Posaunen. Der Einsatz der 2. Trompete, zwei Takte später, ist gleichfalls mit »*p*« bezeichnet. Dieser überraschende Widerspruch wird durch das Autograph nur zum Teil beseitigt, insofern hier der Einsatz der 1. Trompete das erwartete »*f*« hat, der Einsatz der 2. Trompete dagegen ohne dynamische Bezeichnung geblieben ist. Da der *p*-Einsatz der 2. Trompete, wie ihn die Vorlage hat, beabsichtigt sein kann, wurde er nicht, wie es in der 1. Trompete geschah, geändert.

S. 28. In der gedruckten Vorlage heißen im 4., 6. und 7. Takt die alleinstehenden Achtel (auf der 2. Hälfte des jedesmaligen zweiten Taktviertels) in den beiden Violinen . Da es aber zweifellos im 32tel Tremolando weitergeht, wurde diese Form geändert, wie es korrekt ist, in .

* * *

www.ingramcontent.com/pod-product-compliance
Lightning Source LLC
Chambersburg PA
CBHW081327040426
42453CB00013B/2316